CRIME SCIENCE

CYBERCRIME

Leon Gray

Gareth Stevens
Publishing

Please visit our website, www.garethstevens.com. For a free color catalog of all our high-quality books, call toll free 1-800-542-2595 or fax 1-877-542-2596.

Library of Congress Cataloging-in-Publication Data

Grey, Leon.
Cybercrime / by Leon Grey.
  p. cm. — (Crime science)
Includes index.
ISBN 978-1-4339-9485-2 (pbk.)
ISBN 978-1-4339-9486-9 (6-pack)
ISBN 978-1-4339-9484-5 (library binding)
1. Computer crimes — Juvenile literature. I. Title.
HV6773.G46 2014
364.16'8—dc23

First Edition

Published in 2014 by
Gareth Stevens Publishing
111 East 14th Street, Suite 349
New York, NY 10003

© 2014 Gareth Stevens Publishing

Produced by Calcium, www.calciumcreative.co.uk
Designed by Keith Williams and Paul Myerscough
Edited by Sarah Eason and Jennifer Sanderson

Photo credits: Cover: Shutterstock: Balefire t, Dudarev Mikhail b. Inside: Dreamstime: Arrow 4b, Danieloizo 25b, Directphoto 19b, Nyul 17, Suljo 36t; NASA: 35t; Shutterstock: 1000 Words 4t, 41l, 41r, Africa Studio 30, Andresr 36b, Arindambanerjee 42, Atm2003 12, Auremar 10, Bannosuke 32, BasPhoto 43, Conrado 5, Corepics VOF 13, Cristi K 33, De Mango 28, Songquan Deng 35c, Dotshock 24, Helga Esteb 39b, Many Godbehear 38, Goodluz 34, Darrin Henry 29, Jakub Krechowicz 27, Lighthunter 20, Ilike 16r, JMiks 16l, Maga 22, Minerva Studio 18, Monkey Business Images 21, 31b, 39t, Northfoto 37, Odua Images 6, 23, Thomas Pajot 31t, Pavel L Photo and Video 14, Valerie Potapova 25t, Pressmaster 15, Redwall 44, Daniel Schweinert 11, Scyther5 40, Seewhatmitchsee 9, Konstantin Sutyagin 8, Tlorna 1, 45, Angela Waye 26, YanLev 7; Wikimedia Commons: Vincent Diamante 19t.

Printed in the United States of America

CPSIA compliance information: Batch #CS13GS: For further information contact Gareth Stevens, New York, New York at 1-800-542-2595.

CONTENTS

CYBERCRIME

Modern criminals are using computers and the Internet to commit a new type of high-tech crime, called cybercrime. This is a serious crime that costs organizations billions of dollars every year.

Remember, only share information on social networking sites with people you trust.

Crime on Computers

Cybercrime is any type of criminal activity that involves computers and the Internet. Today, many people use computers to browse the Internet and do everyday tasks, such as shopping, studying, and working. Many people also log on to social media sites, such as Twitter and Facebook. Criminals are finding new ways of using technology to carry out crimes. It is the job of the police and computer forensic scientists to fight criminals and solve cybercrimes.

Most people do not realize they have become victims of cybercrime until it is too late.

A Growing Problem

Cybercrime is a big problem. In 2009, the US government suggested that criminal activities in the virtual world cost all the countries around the world combined a staggering $1 trillion. Since many people do not report cybercrimes, the actual figure could even be much higher.

Shocking Statistics

In 2012, the computer security company Norton published some shocking facts. They announced that more than 18 people around the world fell victim to some type of cybercrime every second. This adds up to more than 1.5 million cases of cybercrime every day. More crimes are now taking place on the Internet than on the streets.

BACK IN THE LAB

Many countries now have teams of "cybercops" to combat the growing problem of cybercrime. Back in the laboratory, or lab as it is known, highly trained computer forensic scientists use computers to solve cybercrimes and put the cybercriminals behind bars.

CHAPTER ONE
WHAT IS CYBERCRIME?

People use the term "cybercrime" to describe any type of crime that takes place using computers, smartphones, or the Internet. Cybercrime is now the biggest threat to public security. It is a worldwide problem because of the incredibly rapid development of the Internet.

Computer Crimes

Some cybercriminals are computer experts who secretly break into the computer systems of people and companies. This is known as hacking (see pages 14–15). Other criminals use computers to commit crimes such as money laundering and fraud.

Money laundering involves buying goods and services on the Internet using money gained from other criminal activities. Fraud includes phishing and retail fraud (see pages 30–31). Often, the criminals set up Internet scams to steal information such as bank account details and personal information from other Internet users.

Criminals use computers to steal private information such as credit card details.

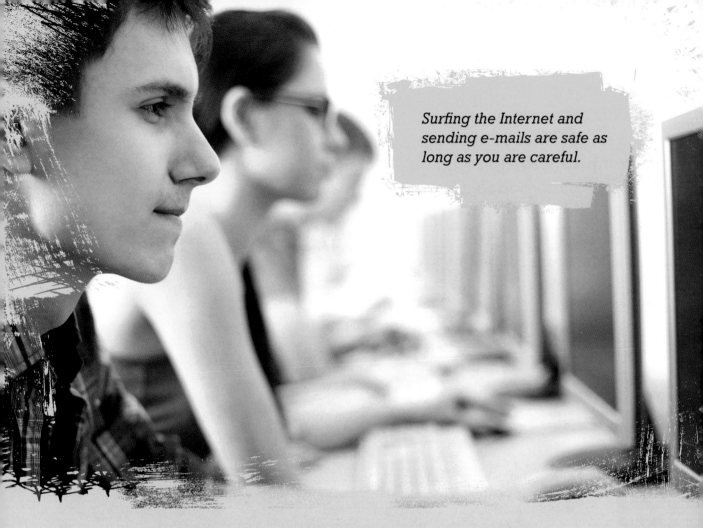

Surfing the Internet and sending e-mails are safe as long as you are careful.

High-profile Cybercrime

Cyberterrorism is one of the greatest cybercrime problems (see pages 42–43). Some terrorists plan their activities and share their ideas with other people in chat rooms on the Internet. Other terrorists are computer experts who target the computers of governments and the military.

CRACKED

Computer forensic experts use their computer skills to search for e-mails and other evidence hidden on a suspect's computer. Computers can hold so much information that a forensic examination may take several months to complete.

HIGH-TECH CRIME

Most cybercriminals are experts who use computers to target their victims and commit crime. They use complex ways to avoid being caught, challenging the skills of the police and computer forensic scientists.

Committing Crimes

Criminals use computers to commit crimes in many different ways. Some are computer experts who use computers to write programs to hack into computer networks and websites. Others use computers to send "junk" e-mail to people to trick them into giving away private information, such as bank account details. This is known as spamming.

Many hackers use their skills to break into computer networks and steal private information.

CRACKED

Computers have become invaluable tools for modern criminals. However, the police are using computers to catch these criminals at their own game. Computer forensic scientists can get useful information from laptop computers, smartphones, and websites and use it as evidence in court.

Cybercriminals are experts who can crack the complex code computers use to store information.

Internet Vandals

Some cybercriminals deliberately target and try to damage other people's computers and websites. Sometimes they attack websites so that they do not work properly. Many companies rely on their websites to do business, so any "downtime" (shutting down the site to repair damage) means that their business loses money. For large businesses, the loss of income can run into many thousands of dollars.

Worms and Viruses

Some criminals write destructive computer programs called viruses and worms. These programs spread around the Internet by e-mail and "infect" millions of computers. Some criminals simply write these programs for fun, to see how far they can spread. Sometimes, the viruses and worms themselves do not damage computers, but they can cause problems by overloading the Internet with information.

CHAPTER TWO
IN THE LAB

Computer forensic scientists use many different techniques to track down cybercriminals. These scientists are experts who examine computers and the files they contain in a laboratory to trace crimes that have taken place on them.

Computer Forensics

A computer forensic scientist is a highly trained computer expert. This person analyzes computers and other electronic devices, extracts information stored on these devices, and then records all the evidence they have found for use in court.

A forensic scientist removes the hard drive of a computer to gather evidence.

Leaving Trails

When criminals commit crimes using computers, they leave trails of their activities on the computer's hard drive. One of the forensic expert's main jobs is to recover this evidence. The problem is that many criminals are computer experts, too, and they are very good at hiding the evidence of their crimes.

BACK IN THE LAB

Forensic experts follow strict rules to ensure evidence is recorded in the right way. This is called the chain of evidence. For example, a detective might find a computer at a suspect's house. The detective must record exactly where he or she found the computer. Then the detective must take the computer back to the lab to be examined.

It can take many weeks to recover the electronic files on a suspect's computer.

What Evidence?

Forensic experts recover many different types of evidence on computers and other electronic devices. For example, text messages and voicemails on a cell phone might place a suspect at the scene of a crime. Criminals may store details of their activities as electronic files on a computer.

PRESERVING THE EVIDENCE

Forensic scientists must preserve the evidence they find on a computer so that it can be used in court. The problem is that opening a computer file to inspect the contents actually changes the file and tampers with the evidence as a result.

Taking a Copy

In the early days of computer forensics, many cases were lost in the courtroom because lawyers challenged the evidence. They argued that the evidence from computers was unreliable because it is so easy to change the files. Today, computer forensic scientists make a complete copy of the computer's hard drive. Then they analyze the copy without changing the original files.

Anti-Forensics

Many criminals are computer experts themselves and know about computer forensic techniques. These criminals have started to use programs called anti-forensics to hide their activities on computers.

Forensic experts document evidence from a suspect's computer to ensure it can be used in court.

Anti-forensics programs make it difficult to recover the information held on a computer.

BACK IN THE LAB

Protecting Information

Some anti-forensics programs erase the files on a computer if anyone other than the owner tries to access them. Others change information about when a file was created or changed. Still others hide sensitive files by storing them inside bigger files or by dividing the files into smaller sections and attaching information to other computer files.

In the past, one scientist could analyze all the files on a computer because a hard drive could not store much information. A modern computer is far more powerful. It can store hundreds of gigabytes of data—the digital equivalent of an entire library. It can take a team of forensic experts months to record and analyze all the information on one computer.

CHAPTER THREE
COMPUTER HACKING

The term "hacking" means breaking into a computer system or website of a person or an organization without permission. Some people hack for fun. Others are criminals with more serious intentions.

Hackers and Hacking

Hackers are cybervandals who break into websites and computer systems and damage them—either for fun or to commit crimes such as fraud. All hacking is a crime. It damages computer networks and websites around the world, causing billions of dollars of damage.

Recreational hackers share their ideas and skills with others at conferences.

Some companies employ "white hats" to protect their computer systems from criminal hackers.

CRACKED

Hackers may encrypt or encode files on their computers so no one else can read them. It is the job of the computer forensic expert to crack these codes so that they can recover the evidence. Then they record all the evidence for lawyers to use in court.

On the Rise

Hacking became a serious problem in the mid-1990s when the number of people using the Internet began to increase dramatically. Hackers could target more computer users and big companies. They could also use the Internet to share tips and coordinate attacks on computer networks or websites. Serious criminals then realized that the Internet could be used to steal money and break the law. The use of the Internet for serious crime had begun.

Hacking for Fun

Many hackers are computer experts who hack into websites and computer networks for the thrill of it. They enjoy the challenge of breaking into a computer system. Many hackers even own up to their illegal activities and point out the security gaps to the companies involved. Many companies now hire these so-called "recreational hackers" to test the security of their computers. The computer hackers who help companies in this way are known as "white hats."

15

HACK ATTACK

Hackers work by gathering information about a target and then finding weaknesses in the security of their computer system. Hackers use high-tech methods to break into computer systems so, as a result, companies have had to rapidly develop tools to improve the security of their computer networks.

Black Hats

Criminal hackers are called "black hats." Some black hats damage websites, delete files, and disrupt the flow of information through the Internet. Others hack into computers to steal valuable information, such as bank account details and credit-card numbers. Expert hackers can also hack into the networks of businesses and banks to steal money.

Hackers use the Internet to attack computer systems and commit their crimes.

Tools for the Job

Hackers use many different tools and techniques to break into computer systems. Computers receive information through data channels called ports. Hackers use devices called port scanners to detect open ports, and then break into the computer without the user detecting them.

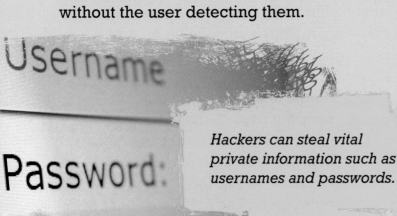

Hackers can steal vital private information such as usernames and passwords.

Victims are often unaware that their computers have been hacked into.

Finding Passwords

Hackers can also install computer programs called keystroke loggers onto a computer without the computer's owner knowing. The hacker can then detect which keys the user is pressing on the keyboard, which might reveal private information such as a password. The hacker can then use this password to take control of the computer. Other tools used by hackers include password crackers that use computer programs to figure out users' passwords.

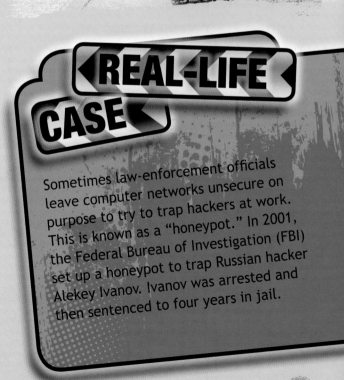

REAL-LIFE CASE

Sometimes law-enforcement officials leave computer networks unsecure on purpose to try to trap hackers at work. This is known as a "honeypot." In 2001, the Federal Bureau of Investigation (FBI) set up a honeypot to trap Russian hacker Alekey Ivanov. Ivanov was arrested and then sentenced to four years in jail.

17

TRACKING THE HACKERS

Although most hackers are computer experts who know how to cover their tracks, they can still leave clues that can be traced by forensic experts.

Internet Tracing

One of the easiest ways to trace a hacker is to find out the Internet Protocol (IP) address of the computer he or she is using. An IP address is a unique sequence of numbers used to identify every computer connected to the Internet. The problem is that hackers often commit their crimes using a complex network of hacked computers. Even the most talented forensic examiner may find it difficult to follow the trail of hacked computers all the way to the original source.

Scientists use the Internet to follow the trail of clues leading to a hacker.

Stopping Hackers

One of the best ways to stop criminals from hacking into a computer is to use a firewall. A firewall stops hackers, as well as harmful programs such as viruses and worms (see pages 20–21), from accessing a computer.

In Japan, supporters of a hacker group called Anonymous demonstrate against the country's strict hacking laws.

Hacker Organizations

Some criminal hackers try to hide from the authorities by operating within hacker groups, which consist mainly of recreational hackers. The criminal hackers benefit from safety in numbers, as well as learn tips from other members of the group.

WE ARE ANONYMOUS

WE ARE LEGION

WE DO NOT FORGIVE

WE DO NOT FORGET

EXPECT US.

REAL-LIFE CASE

In 2009, high-profile American criminal Alberto Gonzalez was jailed for 15 years for cybercrimes including hacking and fraud. Gonzalez hacked into computer networks to steal bank account details and sold the information to other criminals. Gonzalez earned millions of dollars from his crimes. In fact, when they arrested Gonzalez, detectives were amazed to find more than $1 million in cash buried in his parents' backyard.

CHAPTER FOUR
INFECTING COMPUTERS

Many cybercriminals use computer programs to damage computers and disrupt websites. These programs are called malware—short for "malicious software." Other programs, called spyware, infect computers and spy on the users so that criminals can find out private information such as passwords. Software companies now sell programs that can be used to stop these attacks.

Spreading Infection

Computer viruses and worms are malware that spread from computer to computer through the Internet, often in e-mail messages. These programs "infect" computers, affecting how they work and causing very expensive damage.

Using devices such as a USB flash drive is another way to spread malicious software between computers.

Viral Damage

Most viruses infect e-mail programs such as Microsoft Outlook Express. Some viruses hide in computer files or spread through the Internet. The virus causes problems by damaging computers and deleting important files.

Computer viruses are frustrating because they can delete important files and damage computers.

Melissa

One of the most damaging viruses was a program called Melissa, which started infecting computers in 1999. The virus, created by David Smith, hid inside computer files sent by e-mail. Forensic experts tracked down Smith just one week after he released the virus. He was put on trial and then sent to jail for 20 months.

Computer Worms

Programs that infect computers by invading gaps in computer ports are called worms. The worm makes a copy of itself to infect the computer and damage files. The worm then moves on to infect other computers.

REAL-LIFE CASE

In 2005, a German student called Sven Jaschan wrote a computer program that created the devastating Sasser worm. This worm spread through the Internet and damaged millions of computers around the world. Jaschan was just 17 years old, so he was too young to go to jail.

SPYWARE AND TROJAN HORSES

Cybercriminals use programs called spyware and Trojan horses to snoop on computer users and even take control of their computers. The criminals then steal personal information, such as bank account details and passwords, and sell this information to other criminals.

Spies in Computers

Spyware is any type of computer software that hides on a computer and spies on the computer user, collecting personal details. The spyware author records this information and sells it to companies that advertise goods and services based on the sites the user has visited. Some spyware is packaged with adware, which is software that displays unwanted Internet advertisements to people without their permission.

A cybercriminal secretly spies on his victim to see what he or she is doing on the Internet.

Spyware can be used to log keystrokes, revealing private information such as credit card details.

Internet Spies

Criminals often use spyware to steal credit-card numbers, bank details, and passwords. Some types of spyware record a user's keystrokes to reveal secret passwords. Others take screenshots of the user's computer screen to reveal private information. The criminals use this information to commit other crimes, such as Internet fraud and identity theft.

Trojan Horses

A Trojan horse is a computer program that claims to do one thing but really does something completely different. Hackers use Trojans to access and damage computer networks. Trojans cannot spread from computer to computer in the same way as worms and viruses, but they can still cause a lot of damage.

REAL-LIFE CASE

Forensic experts use spyware to catch criminals at their own game. In 2007, FBI computer experts used top-secret spyware to trap a teenager called Josh Glazebrook. Glazebrook had sent bomb threats to his high school by e-mail. He was jailed for 90 days for his crime.

23

SAFETY FIRST!

Viruses, worms, spyware, and Trojans are such a big problem that companies have developed programs to protect computers. Many people also use encryption tools and firewalls to protect their computers.

Scanning for Infection

Antivirus software stops viruses and worms from infecting computers. The software scans all the files on the computer's hard drive to see if there is a virus. If the antivirus software detects a virus, it deletes it or moves it into a folder where it cannot do any harm. Criminals are releasing new viruses and worms all the time, so antivirus software must be updated.

Many companies employ experts to check computer networks for malicious software such as viruses.

Firewalls

A firewall is a computer program that stops viruses, worms, and Trojans from entering a computer and causing damage. It also prevents hackers from accessing a computer. The firewall checks any data coming into the computer, such as e-mails or Internet files. If the firewall detects harmful files, it stops them from entering the computer.

Use a secure password and encryption software to protect the information on your computer.

You can download antivirus software for free on the Internet.

AVG Free - Antivirus Download

AVG.
Free Anti-Virus

Get Protection   Supp

Homep

Encryption

Many computers come with built-in encryption software. Encryption is a way of scrambling data on a computer so no one other than the owner of the computer can read it. The owner uses a special "key" or password to unlock the encrypted files on their computer.

CRACKED

When a hacker tries to access a computer that is protected by a firewall, a log records what happens. The log is a "diary" that shows how and when the hacker tried to break into the system. The log records useful information, such as an IP address, so forensic experts can identify the hackers.

25

CHAPTER FIVE

SPAMMING

Spam is any e-mail message a person receives without asking for it. Spam can be a simple message sent to advertise legal products. It can also be a message sent by a criminal to steal private information and trick people out of cash.

Spam and Spamming

Almost everyone with an e-mail account will receive spam. Some companies send spam e-mails to advertise their goods. This junk e-mail is a nuisance but it is fairly harmless. Criminals use spam to steal information and money, and send malware such as worms and viruses.

Many companies use spam perfectly legally to sell products and services.

Danger by E-mail

People who send spam e-mail are called spammers. They send hundreds of millions of e-mails every day, which block e-mail accounts and flood the Internet with unwanted information. In 2009, almost 90 percent of all the e-mails sent were spam. Most spam comes from the United States, but spammers in other countries, such as China, are now catching up.

Spam Traps

Forensic experts use false e-mail addresses to trap the criminals who send spam. Criminals use programs called e-mail–address harvesters to troll the Internet on the lookout for e-mail addresses. So forensic experts publish false e-mails on webpages and then wait for spam to arrive. The forensics team then tries to identify the source of the spam using the IP address of the sender.

REAL-LIFE CASE

In 2008, a spammer named Robert Soloway was sent to jail for four years. He was nicknamed the "Spam King" because he was sending millions of spam e-mails around the world. Soloway used spam to infect computers with viruses, commit identity theft, and steal millions of dollars from his unsuspecting victims.

27

BOTNETS

Computer criminals can take control of huge computer networks. They infect the computers with worms and viruses and then use them to attack websites or send millions of spam e-mails. These computer networks are known as botnets, or zombie networks.

Robot Networks

The word "botnet" is short for "robot network," and each computer on the network is called a "zombie computer." A botnet may contain up to 20,000 zombie computers. Hackers usually take control of computers by sending out junk e-mails. When a person opens up the e-mail, they unknowingly download a virus or worm. Some hackers use peer-to-peer (P2P) networks (see pages 36–37), where people share music files, images, or hyperlinks on websites to infect computers.

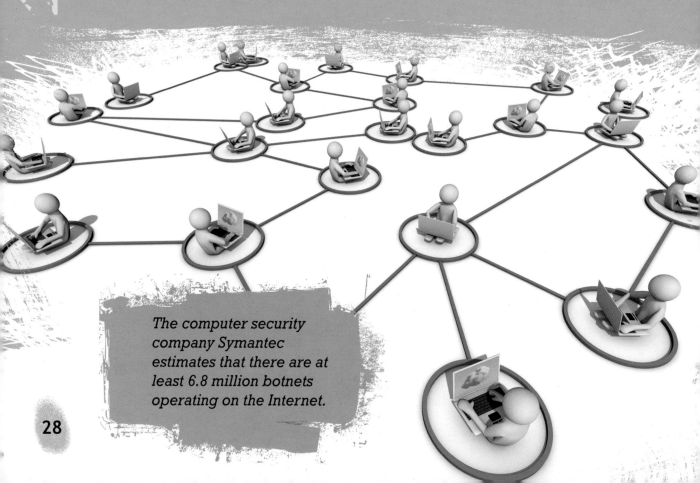

The computer security company Symantec estimates that there are at least 6.8 million botnets operating on the Internet.

Your computer will still work if it is part of a botnet, but criminals can also use it to commit crime.

Taking Control

Once a virus has infected a computer, the hacker takes control. Most people do not realize their computer is part of a botnet. But every time they switch on the machine, the hacker is using it to send out junk e-mails and commit crimes.

Cyber Army

The botnet is like an army of computers, all under the control of the hacker. Some companies pay hackers to send spam e-mails advertising their products. Criminals also pay hackers to distribute viruses, worms, and other malicious computer programs.

REAL-LIFE CASE

In 2010, the FBI and detectives from Spain and Slovenia arrested a 26-year-old hacker known as "Iserdo." Iserdo created one of the biggest botnets, affecting more then 13 million computers in 190 countries around the world. He used the botnet to steal credit-card details and bank passwords. It took forensic experts more than three years to trace Iserdo, who is now in jail.

CHAPTER SIX

FRAUD ON THE WEB

Whenever someone turns on their computer and surfs the Internet they are at risk of fraud. Criminals steal information, such as bank account details, or take money directly from banks. Fraud also includes Internet piracy, where criminals sell illegal copies of music or movies.

Internet Fraud

Cybercriminals use many different techniques to steal information and trick people out of their money. Some advertise products that do not exist, while others sell goods such as fake designer clothes.

Some criminals use the Internet to sell fake or stolen goods.

Con Artists

Many companies sell their products on the Internet. Like the stores in your local shopping mall, most of them are genuine traders. But some sites are run by criminals who are out to con you.

CRACKED

Many criminals have programs known as anti-forensics on the computers they use to commit fraud. Anti-forensics programs make it harder for investigators to find evidence stored on a hard drive. Detectives must disable these programs before they can look at the files hidden away on the computer.

Criminals can make a lot of money by influencing the price of stocks and shares.

Bogus Sellers

Some criminals set up bogus websites that offer people goods that are much cheaper than elsewhere. Shoppers buy the goods and pay for them by credit card but the goods never arrive. The criminals sell the credit-card details to other criminals or use them to run up huge debts. Other criminals sell from genuine websites such as eBay, but ship fake or stolen goods instead of the real thing.

Investment Fraud

Another type of fraud involves speculating on the stock market. This is where criminals spread false rumors to influence the price of stocks. The criminals buy the stocks at the lowest price and sell them when the price rises again. Investigators are constantly looking out for people making large sums of money on the stock market in case they are committing investment fraud.

PHISHING

Some criminals set up complex scams that trick people into giving away personal information, such as bank account passwords. The criminals then use these details to steal money.

Fakes on the Internet

One of the most common Internet scams is "phishing" (pronounced "fishing"). In this scam, cybercriminals create bogus websites and then send out spam, which directs people to the fake site. The bogus site could be a copy of a genuine online bank and looks exactly like the real site. The site invites the unsuspecting user to enter personal details such as a password. Criminals then use these details to access the real site and empty the victim's bank account.

Login

Criminals use phishing scams to steal private information such as your username and password.

Username:

Password:

☐ Forget Password?   ☐ Remember Passwo

 Login   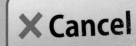 ✕ Cancel

Anyone can fall victim to a phishing scam. Never reveal private information if you suspect that an e-mail is fake.

Common Crime

Phishing is a common cybercrime. Millions of Internet users are duped out of money every year. However, it is easy to spot this type of Internet scam. Genuine companies never ask customers for personal details such as whole passwords.

On the Case

Cybercriminals are getting much better at phishing and investigators face a constant challenge to keep up with them. As soon the forensic experts identify and remove one bogus site, another appears in its place. Investigators from many countries now work together to identify the criminal gangs behind these scams.

COMPANY CYBERCRIME

Cybercriminals also target big businesses to commit crimes. Expert hackers can break into high-security sites, such as banks, to steal money and information which they sell to other criminals.

Closing In

Cybercriminals target companies in many different ways. Some steal money directly, while others take information, such as designs for new products. The criminals then blackmail the company, threatening to sell their ideas to rival companies unless they pay the criminals large sums of money.

Inside Job

Even the most experienced hacker would find it hard to hack into a bank. Most banks spend millions of dollars on high-tech security measures to prevent such attacks. Cyberattacks usually take place with help from people "on the inside"—people who actually work for the bank.

Some criminals pay employees to help them hack into their company's computer system to steal valuable information.

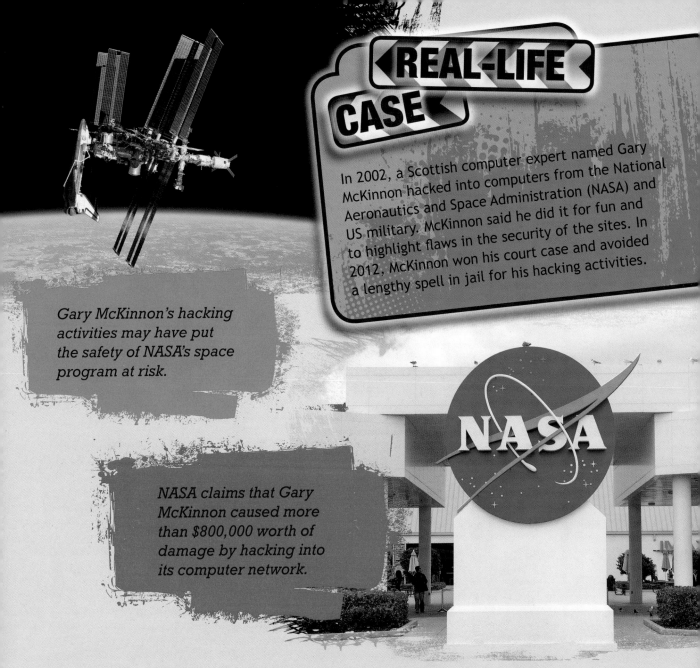

In 2002, a Scottish computer expert named Gary McKinnon hacked into computers from the National Aeronautics and Space Administration (NASA) and US military. McKinnon said he did it for fun and to highlight flaws in the security of the sites. In 2012, McKinnon won his court case and avoided a lengthy spell in jail for his hacking activities.

Gary McKinnon's hacking activities may have put the safety of NASA's space program at risk.

NASA claims that Gary McKinnon caused more than $800,000 worth of damage by hacking into its computer network.

Revenge Attacks

In some cases, the criminals are ex-employees, who target companies in revenge attacks. These people may have been fired or laid off by their old organization, and hold a grudge against it. Angry ex-employees use their inside knowledge to hack into the company's computer network and delete important files.

Catching the Criminals

When businesses fall victim to hackers, detectives often do background checks on workers and ex-employees to see if anyone might have reason to commit the crime. Sometimes, the investigators use similar tactics to the criminals themselves, setting up their own bogus websites with security flaws to reel in the criminals.

PIRATES ON THE WEB

One of the most common types of Internet fraud is piracy. This is when criminals sell fake copies of music, movies, and computer games. Sometimes people then share these "pirate" copies, which makes the problem even worse.

Breaking the Law

Criminals are making billions of dollars every year selling pirate copies of music, movies, and computer software. Piracy is illegal. In most countries, there are laws to protect musicians, moviemakers, and the people who make computer games and software. These laws are supposed to stop people from copying their work, but the criminals ignore them.

Musicians lose money every time someone downloads pirate copies of their songs and videos.

Downloading music from the Internet is legal as long as you use a genuine online music store.

CRACKED

Forensic experts regularly check P2P networks and the people who use them. They trace the IP addresses of any users who regularly log in to these sites and download large files. The experts examine downloads to see if they are pirate copies and then identify the users by contacting their Internet Service Provider (ISP).

Napster is an online music store that started life as a P2P network.

Internet Downloads

Many people download music and movies from the Internet. Users pay a fee every time they download a song or watch a movie on the Internet. The websites that offer these services are genuine. Other sites, called peer-to-peer (P2P) networks, let people share files with each other. While these sites are sometimes used for sharing personal photos and video clips, they are also used illegally to share pirate copies of music and movies. Sharing pirate material on P2P networks is against the law.

Cheap, Yet Poor

Some people buy pirate copies of music and movies because they are much cheaper than the genuine items, but they do not realize that the quality of pirate copies is often very poor in comparison to the legitimate, legal version.

CHAPTER SEVEN
ONLINE BULLIES

Some people use the Internet to bully people and send them threatening messages. This is called cyberbullying, and it is now against the law in many countries.

Cyberbullying

Online bullying is a big problem among young people. The bullies target their unfortunate victims in different ways. Some send nasty e-mails and instant messages, while others make offensive comments in chat rooms and online blogs.

Cruelty via the Internet

Online bullies are no different from the bullies found in playgrounds. Most of them use e-mail, chat rooms, blogs, and websites to send their offensive messages, while hiding behind the Internet. These people may think they are funny, but they may be breaking the law.

Internet bullying is exactly the same as doing it in person. How would you feel if someone bullied you?

Cyberstalking

Sometimes cyberbullying can develop into cyberstalking. This happens when the bullies send e-mailed threats, chat-room posts that are abusive, and other messages over and over again. This can become more serious when the cyberbullying spills over into the rest of their life, and the bullies follow up their threats with violence.

Catching Bullies

Any messages kept by victims of cyberbullying can be used as evidence. The messages may help to identify who is responsible as they might contain words, phrases, or other clues that could reveal the identity of the bully.

People use smartphones to send texts and instant messages to their friends. This has made the problem of cyberbullying worse.

REAL-LIFE CASE

In 1999, American actress Gwyneth Paltrow became the victim of a cyberstalker named Dante Soiu. Soiu became obsessed with the actress and bombarded her with letters and e-mails. Soiu was arrested after his online threats turned into physical harassment. In 2000, the Californian courts declared Soiu to be insane, and he was sent to a mental hospital.

SOCIAL MEDIA

Social media sites, such as Facebook, Twitter and MySpace, have become an everyday part of life. Many people use them to communicate with friends and post comments about themselves. For some, the line between private and public life is becoming blurred, and cybercriminals are now taking advantage of this.

Helping to Catch Criminals

Social media sites may seem harmless, but they can help criminals to commit crimes. People may post private information about themselves, such as their address, telephone number, and date of birth. Criminals use this information to commit identity theft and other crimes.

Social Media Fraud

Criminals also exploit people's love of social media by flooding the sites with harmful viruses. These viruses work in the same way as those sent by e-mail. The criminals post "friendly" messages on the sites to entice people to download viruses or reveal important private information such as passwords.

Stay safe on social media sites. Never accept a friend request from someone you do not know.

CRACKED

In 2011, riots broke out in London, England, and other cities across the country. Many rioters were arrested when police identified them from Facebook images showing them looting stores. The rioters also used Twitter to plan their attacks and tell other rioters where to meet. The police traced and arrested many rioters by reading their Twitter posts.

Many London rioters hid their faces to avoid being identified by the police.

The police arrested many London rioters thanks to the evidence posted on Facebook and Twitter.

Hacking into Phones

Many people use smartphones instead of computers to shop on the Internet and access their online bank accounts. Criminals hack into the phones using WiFi or simply watch people as they enter their usernames and passwords. This makes it much easier for criminals to commit fraudulent crimes.

Bullying

Social media sites make it easy for bullies to pick on people they do not like in another form of cyberbullying. On some sites, users have posted lies about people and have then been arrested for making these false claims. This form of online bullying now poses a serious challenge for police.

TERRORISM ON THE WEB

Some criminals are turning to a new form of terrorism. They are using their computer skills to hack into government computers and steal secret information. The information is then used to plot terrorist attacks.

Other Techniques

Terrorists also use the Internet in other ways. Some create websites to voice their opinions and recruit new people to their cause. Others use websites to find out information such as the movement of a target or how to build a bomb.

Some criminals use the Internet to plan acts of terrorism.

In 2008, police in India used the evidence from a cell phone and GPS device to convict Mohammed Qasab of bombing the Taj Mahal Palace Hotel in Mumbai.

Cyberwarfare

Some countries are waging digital wars with other countries. This new type of warfare is called "cyberwarfare." Countries use the Internet to spy on their enemies and hack into their computers to find out top-secret information. Some employ former criminal hackers to break into military sites and essential services, such as electricity and water, so that they do not work properly. Cyberwarfare also includes denial-of-service (DOS) attacks, in which hackers flood important government websites with so many e-mails that the website cannot work properly.

REAL-LIFE CASE

In 2007, American Michael Curtis Reynolds was convicted of terrorist crimes. He was caught by FBI agents after admitting to a plot to bomb American oil pipelines in a Yahoo! chat room. Reynolds claimed to be working with the terrorist group Al-Qaeda. He is currently serving 30 years in jail.

THE FUTURE OF CYBERCRIME

Cybercrime is a growing threat. As cybercriminals find new ways to commit their crimes, forensic investigators are matching these new advances. Technology is constantly improving, and criminals and forensic experts are locked in a "cybercrime race" to gain the upper hand.

Using WiFi

WiFi is a wireless access point for the Internet. Many people now use WiFi at home to connect to the Internet. They also use portable electronic devices, such as tablet computers and smartphones, to access the Internet on the move. Public WiFi hotspots make the Internet available everywhere, from airports and coffeehouses to hotels and many other public buildings.

WiFi networks are vulnerable to attack by cybercriminals.

Many people now use smartphones, tablet computers, and laptops to access their private computer files from a "cloud."

Wireless Crime

Criminals are also using WiFi to commit crime. They are hacking into private WiFi networks in people's homes to access the Internet and commit their illegal activities. This is known as "piggybacking." Other criminals commit Internet crime using public WiFi hotspots. Using WiFi, criminals can remain anonymous and commit their crimes from almost anywhere.

Cloud Computing

In cloud computing, information is stored on a virtual server called a "cloud" rather than on a hard drive. Some people think cloud computing will protect people from cybercrime because criminals cannot access their private information. Others think that if the criminals find a way of hacking into the cloud then they can access everyone's information very easily from just one place.

REAL-LIFE CASE

In 2012, Joshuah Witt, John Griffin, and Brad Lowe broke into company computer networks through unsecure WiFi. Then they installed keystroke loggers on computers, which revealed passwords for the companies' bank accounts. It is estimated the three criminals netted more than $3 million before forensic experts managed to trace them.

GLOSSARY

Al-Qaeda an Islamic terrorist organization formed by Osama Bin Ladin

adware computer programs that display advertisements for goods and services on a computer

biometric data unique information, such as a fingerprint, that can be used to identify a person

blogs websites on which people voice their opinions

botnets networks of computers used to send spam or attack websites

chat rooms websites on which people can talk to one another and exchange ideas

convict to find a person guilty of a criminal act

cyberterrorism using computers to cause fear and disruption

data information such as words or images

databases information that is stored on computers

decipher to convert data into something people can understand

digital information that is represented in a number form

download to copy from one computer to another computer

encrypted scrambled into a secret code

evidence information presented to a court

firewall a protective screen that blocks malware such as viruses and worms

fraud deceiving someone for personal gain

hacking accessing computers without permission from the owners

harassment persistent, threatening behavior

identity theft stealing private information to commit fraud

illegal against the law

Internet the global network of computers

launder to use the money gained from criminal activities

malware malicious software, such as viruses or worms, which damages infected computers

military any of the armed forces

peer-to-peer (P2P) networks file-sharing networks found on the Internet

phishing sending e-mails that link to bogus websites

spamming sending unwanted e-mail messages to many people

spyware software that gathers information about people without their knowledge

stock market a financial market, such as the New York Stock Exchange, which sells stocks and shares

Trojan horses programs that appear to be useful but actually damage computers

viruses programs that infect computers and damage them

worms computer programs that copy themselves and then infect computers and damage them

FOR MORE INFORMATION

BOOKS

Gray, Leon. *Solving Cybercrime*. Berkley Heights, NJ: Enslow Publishers, 2009.

Hynson, Colin. *Cyber Crime*. New York, NY: Smart Apple Media, 2012.

Townsend, John. *Cyber Crime Secrets*. Mankato, MN: Amicus, 2012.

WEBSITES

The How Stuff Works website explains how computer forensic scientists hunt for cybercriminals:
**computer.howstuffworks.com/
computer-forensic.htm**

Discover how forensic scientists use computers and virtual-reality technology to map out crime scenes at:
people.howstuffworks.com/vr-csi.htm

Visit the Federal Bureau of Investigation website to find out more about cybercrime at:
www.fbi.gov/cyberinvest/cyberhome.htm

47

INDEX